How to Hold Your Guitar

Hold your guitar in a position that is most comfortable for you. Some positions are shown below.

When playing, keep your left wrist away from the fingerboard. This will allow your fingers to be in a better position to finger the chords. Press your fingers firmly, but make certain they do not touch the neighboring strings.

Tilt the neck slightly up. Don't twist the body of the guitar to see the strings better.

Sitting.

Sitting with legs crossed.

The guitar is strummed with the right hand. You may use a guitar pick or your thumb. Strum all chords in a downward motion unless otherwise indicated.

Standing with strap.

The Right Hand

To *strum* means to play the strings with your right hand by brushing quickly across them. There are two common ways of strumming the strings. One is with a pick, and the other is with your fingers.

Strumming with a Pick

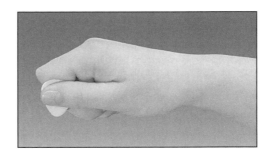

Hold the pick between your thumb and index finger. Hold it firmly, but don't squeeze it too hard.

Strum from the 6th string (the thickest, lowest-sounding string) to the 1st string (the thinnest, highest-sounding string).

Important: Strum by mostly moving your wrist, not just your arm. Use as little motion as possible. Start as close to the top string as you can, and never let your hand move past the edge of the guitar.

Start near the top string.

Move mostly your wrist, not just your arm. Finish near the bottom string.

Strumming with Your Fingers

Decide if you feel more comfortable strumming with the side of your thumb or the nail of your index finger. The strumming motion is the same with the thumb or finger as it is when using the pick.

Strum from the 6th string (the thickest, lowest-sounding string) to the 1st string (the thinnest, highest-sounding string).

Strumming with the thumb.

Strumming with the index finger.

The Left Hand

Proper Left Hand Position

Learning to use your left hand fingers starts with a good hand position. Place your hand so your thumb rests comfortably in the middle of the back of the neck. Position your fingers on the front of the neck as if you are gently squeezing a ball between them and your thumb. Keep your elbow in and your fingers curved.

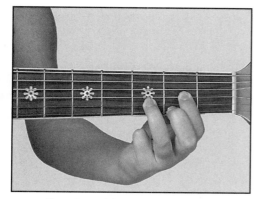

Keep elbow in and fingers curved. Arch your wrist slightly so your fingertips can more easily come down on top of the strings

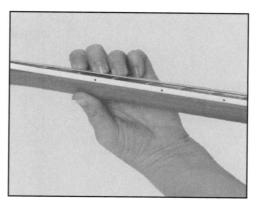

Position fingers as if you are gently squeezing a ball between your fingertips and thumb. Place the thumb under the fingerboard opposite the 2nd finger.

Placing a Finger on a String

When you press a string with a left hand finger, make sure you press firmly with the tip of your finger and as close to the fret wire as you can without actually being right on it. Short fingernails are important! This will create a clean, bright tone.

Right!
Finger presses the string down near the fret without actually being on it.

Wrong!
Finger is too far from fret wire; tone is "buzzy" and indefinite.

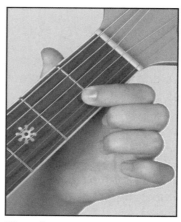

Wrong!
Finger is on top of fret wire; tone is muffled and unclear.

How to Tune Your Guitar to a Keyboard

The six strings of the guitar are the same pitches as the six notes shown on the keyboard in this illustration:

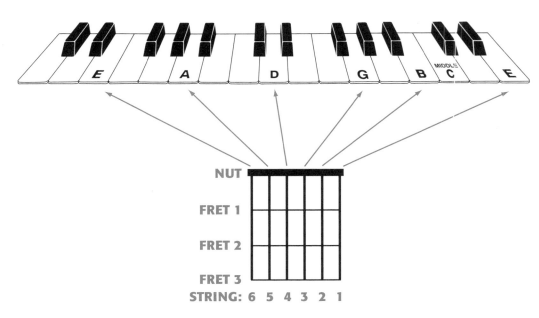

Tuning the Guitar to Itself

Tune the 6th string to E on the keyboard. If no keyboard is available, approximate E as best you can and proceed as follows:

Press 5th fret of 6th string to get pitch of 5th string (A).

Press 5th fret of 5th string to get pitch of 4th string (D).

Press 5th fret of 4th string to get pitch of 3rd string (G).

Press 4th fret of 3rd string to get pitch of 2nd string (B).

Press 5th fret of 2nd string to get pitch of 1st string (E).

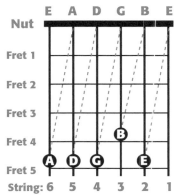

Tuning with the Audio or Video 🔊 Track 1

To tune while listening to the audio or watching the video, listen to the directions and match each of your strings to the corresponding pitches.

How to Read Chord Diagrams

Fingering diagrams show where to place the fingers of your left hand. Strings not played are shown with dashed lines.

The number within the circle indicates the finger that is pressed down.

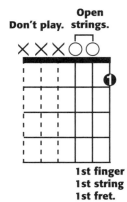

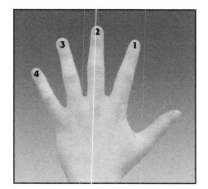

How to Use an Electronic Tuner

An electronic tuner is a handy device that can help keep your guitar in tune. You pick each string one at a time, and the tuner guides you to the exact pitch the string should be in order for it to be in tune. Until your ear becomes more experienced, an electronic tuner can be extremely useful.

Getting Acquainted with Music

Musical sounds are indicated by symbols called *notes*. Their time value is determined by their color (white or black) and by stems or flags attached to the note head.

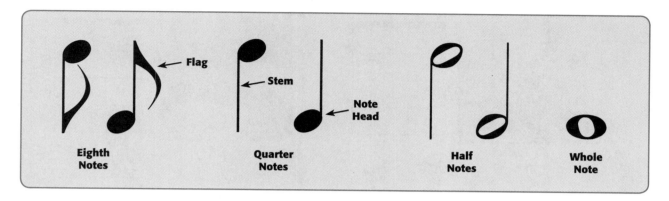

The Staff

The notes are named after the first seven letters of the alphabet (A–G), endlessly repeated to embrace the entire range of musical sound. The name and pitch of the note is determined by its position on five horizontal lines and the spaces between, called the *staff*.

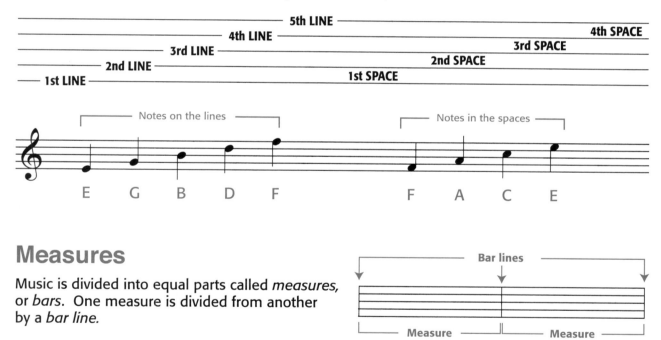

Measures

Music is divided into equal parts called *measures*, or *bars*. One measure is divided from another by a *bar line*.

Clefs

During the evolution of musical notation, the staff had from 2 to 20 lines, and symbols were invented to locate certain lines and the pitch of the note on that line. These symbols are called *clefs*.

Music for guitar is written in the *G clef*, or *treble clef*. Originally, the Gothic letter G was used on a four-line staff to establish the pitch of G.

This grew into the modern notation on a five-line staff:

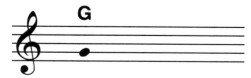

The First String E

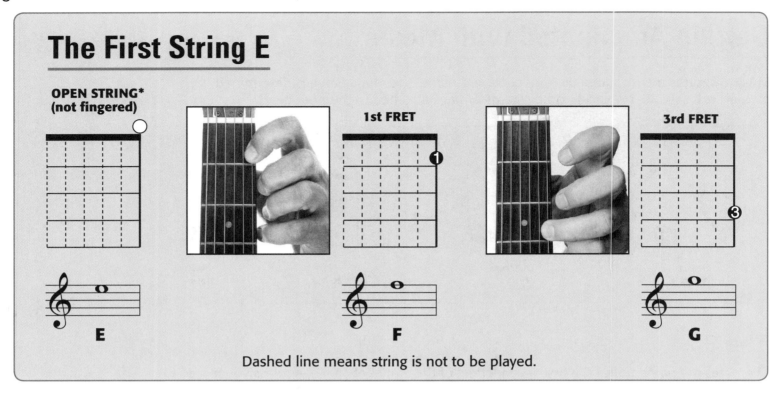

OPEN STRING* (not fingered)

1st FRET

3rd FRET

E   F   G

Dashed line means string is not to be played.

Use only down-strokes indicated by ⊓.
The symbol ○ over a note means *open string.* Do not finger.

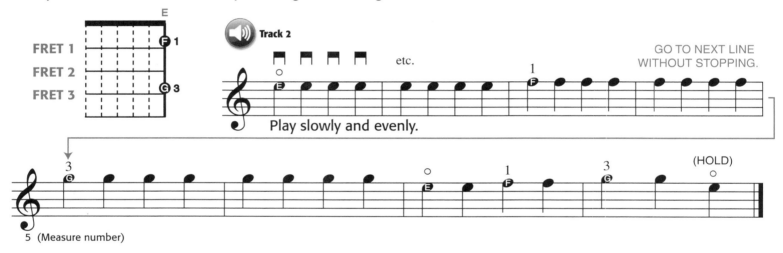

FRET 1
FRET 2
FRET 3

Track 2

etc.

GO TO NEXT LINE
WITHOUT STOPPING.

Play slowly and evenly.

(HOLD)

5 (Measure number)

PLAYING WITH E, F, G   Track 3

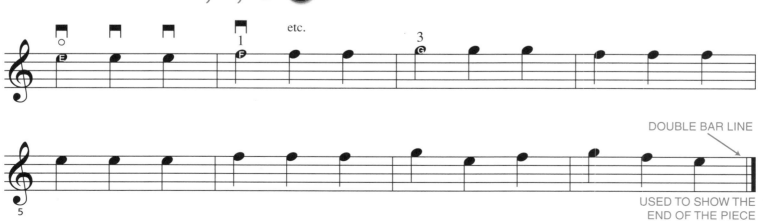

etc.

DOUBLE BAR LINE

USED TO SHOW THE
END OF THE PIECE

5

*Though no photo is shown for the open string, the fingers of the LH should remain slightly above the string to be ready to play the correct fret when needed. The thumb should also remain in its proper position.

MORE 🔊 Track 4

Left hand fingers: When playing from the 1st to the 3rd fret, keep the 1st finger down.
Only the G will sound, but when you go back to F, your playing will sound smoother.

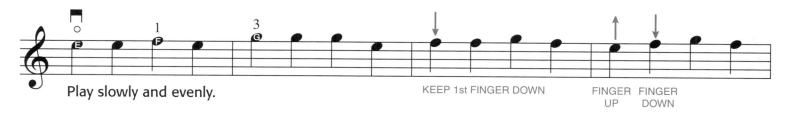

Play slowly and evenly.   KEEP 1st FINGER DOWN   FINGER   FINGER
                                                                                 UP   DOWN

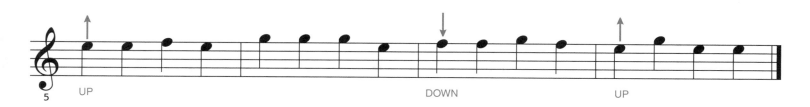

5   UP   DOWN   UP

STILL MORE 🔊 Track 5

Left hand fingers: Place as close to the fret wires as possible without actually touching them.

                                                                    KEEP 1st FINGER DOWN

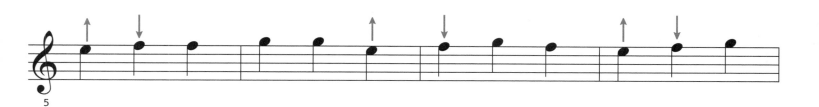

5

9

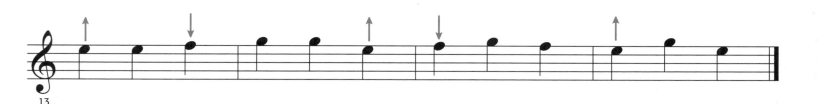

13

No More  **Track 6**

Left hand fingers: Use only the tips—keep them curved.
Left hand thumb: Place on the back of the neck opposite the 1st and 2nd fingers.

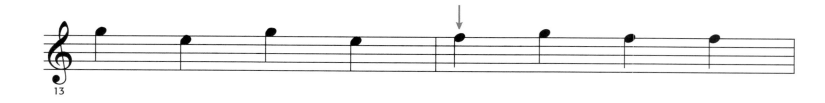

Sound-Off: How to Count Time

Four Kinds of Notes

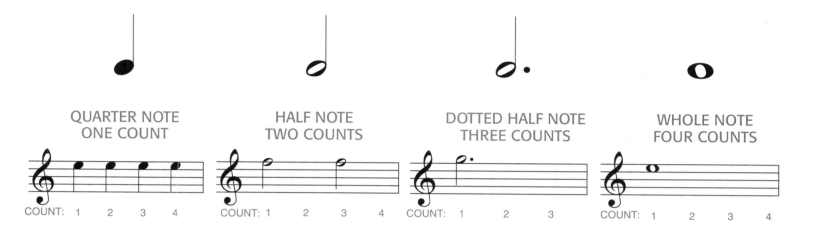

Time Signatures

Each piece of music has numbers at the beginning called a *time signature*. These numbers tell us how to count time.

The TOP NUMBER tells us how many counts are in each measure.
The BOTTOM NUMBER tells us what kind of note gets one count.

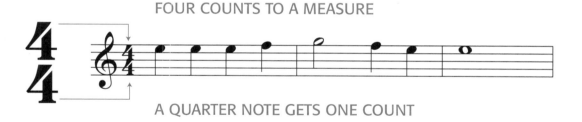

Important: Go back and fill in the missing time signatures of the songs you have already learned.

The Second String B

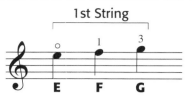

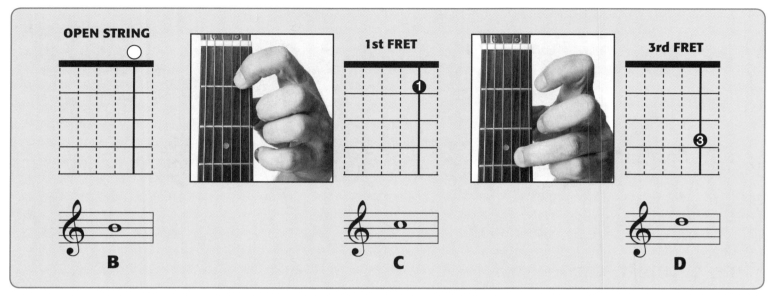

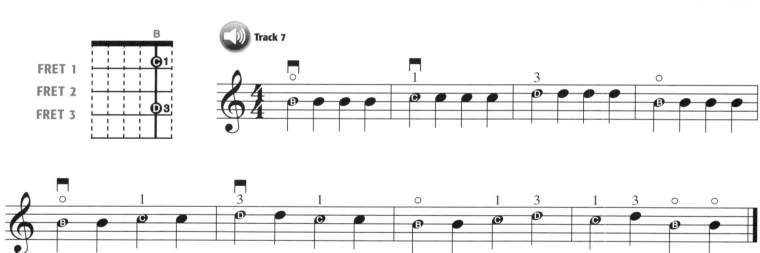

TWO-STRING ROCK   Track 8

MERRY-GO-ROUND  Track 9

BEAUTIFUL BROWN EYES 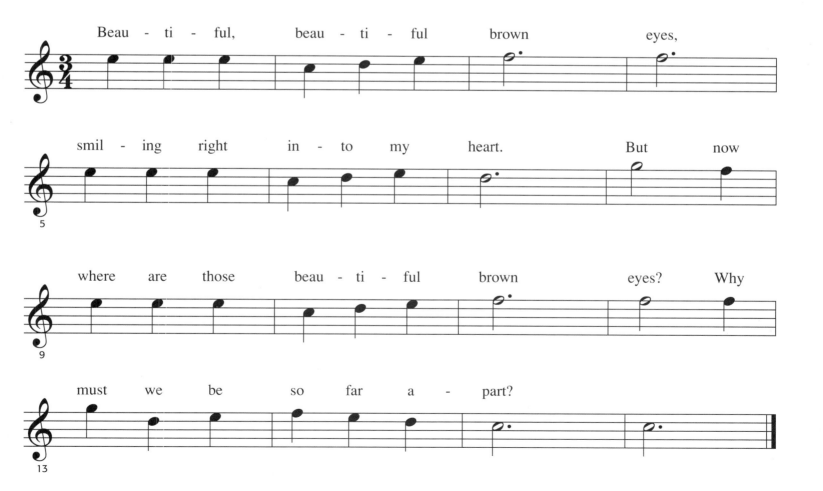 Track 10

GUITAR ROCK 🔊 Track 11

If you have a teacher or a guitar playing friend, the chord symbols above each staff may be used to play a duet (two players). These chords are not to be played by the student.

JINGLE BELLS 🔊 Track 12

ALOUETTE

Track 13

Traditional French-Canadian

The Third String G

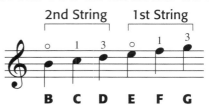

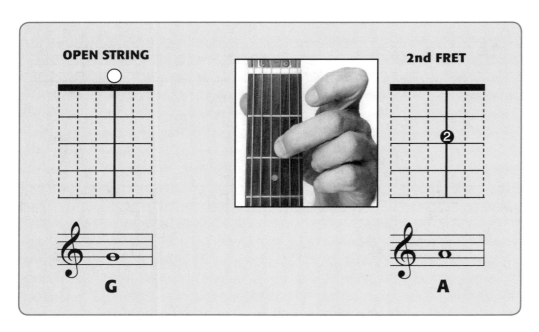

OPEN STRING

G

2nd FRET

A

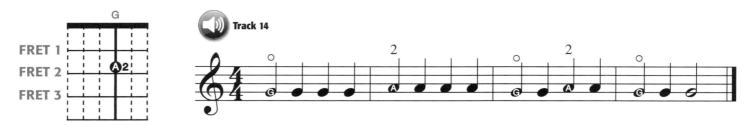

Track 14

AU CLAIR DE LA LUNE Track 15

TEACHER: G   D⁷   G   D⁷   G   D⁷

G   D⁷   G   D⁷

G   D⁷   G

17

THREE-STRING ROCK  Track 16

LARGO 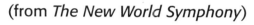 Track 17

(from *The New World Symphony*)

Antonin Dvořák

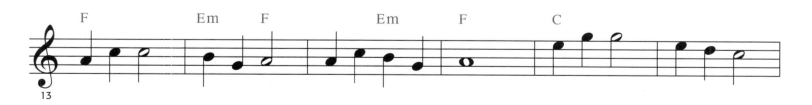

BACK TO THE '50s Track 18

Repeat Signs

The double dots inside the double bars indicate that everything between the double bars must be repeated.

  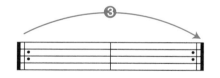

AURA LEE Track 19

Elvis Presley recorded this folk song in a modern version called "Love Me Tender."

Introducing Chords

A *chord* is a combination of harmonious notes. All notes except the whole note have a stem going up or down. When notes are struck together as a chord, they are connected by the same stem.

(Not to be played.)

Chord Study No. 1 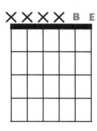 Track 20

This exercise uses two-note chords on the open B and E strings. Play both strings together with one down-stroke.

An x above a string also means that string is not to be played.

Chord Study No. 2 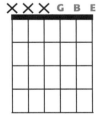 Track 21

This exercise uses three-note chords on the open G, B, and E strings. Learn the order of the strings thoroughly. Play with the wrist free and relaxed. Keep your eyes on the notes and not on the fingerboard.

20

Three-String C Chord

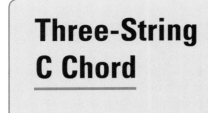

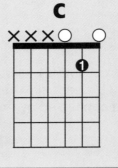

Track 22

(HOLD C DOWN TO THE END OF THE EXERCISE)

Ode to Joy **Track 23**

(Theme from Beethoven's *9th Symphony*)

Ludwig van Beethoven

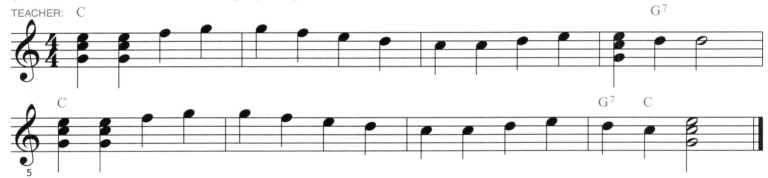

Quarter Rest

This sign indicates silence for one count. For a clearer effect, you may stop the sound of the strings by touching the strings lightly with the heel of the right hand.

Rock 'n' Rhythm **Track 24**

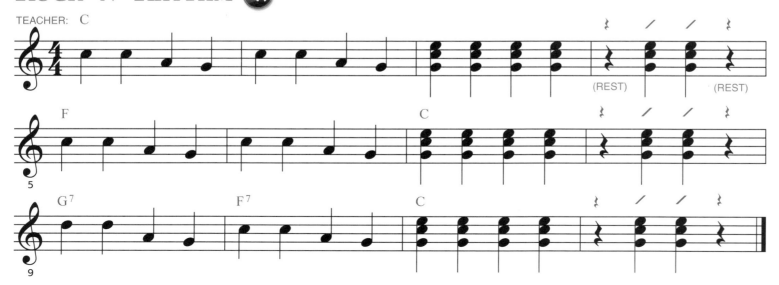

Three-String G7 Chord

Track 25

(HOLD F DOWN TO THE END)

TWO-CHORD ROCK Track 26

LOVE SOMEBODY Track 27

Here is a song for you to sing while you play the accompaniment. The slanting line below or following a chord symbol (C / / / G7 / / /) means to play the same chord for each line. Repeat the chord until a new chord symbol appears.

PLAY: C / / / G⁷ / / / C / / / G⁷ / / /
SING: Love some-bod-y, 'deed I do. Love some-bod-y, now guess who?

C / / / G⁷ / / / C / G⁷ / C / / /
Love some-bod-y have you guessed? You're the one that I love best.

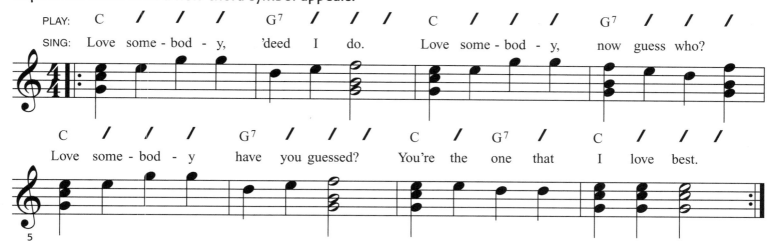

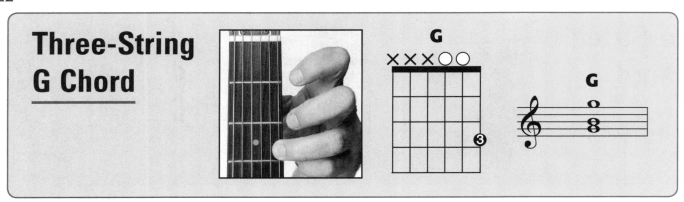

Track 28

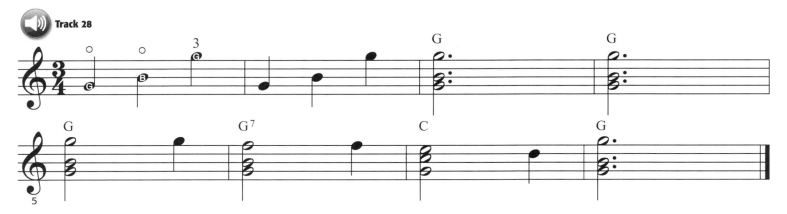

ROCKIN' WITH G & C   Track 29

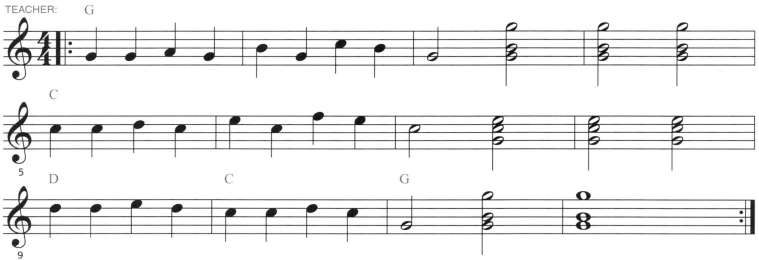

DOWN IN THE VALLEY   Track 30

Play this song as a guitar solo by playing the music, then sing the melody
and accompany yourself by playing the chord line.

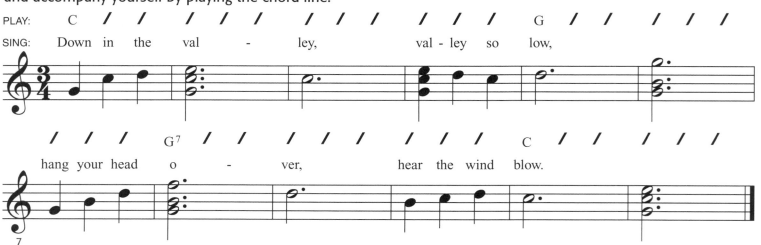

OH, SUSANNA  Track 31

Stephen Foster

TEACHER:

Oh, I came from A - la - ba - ma with a gui - tar on my knee; I'm goin' to Lou - 'si - a - na, my_____ true love for to see. It rained all night the day I left, the weath - er it was dry; the sun so hot I froze to death, Su - san - na don't you cry. Oh, Su - san - na, oh, don't you cry for me, I've come from A - la - ba - ma with a gui - tar on my knee.

The Fourth String D

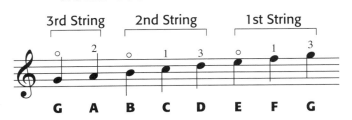

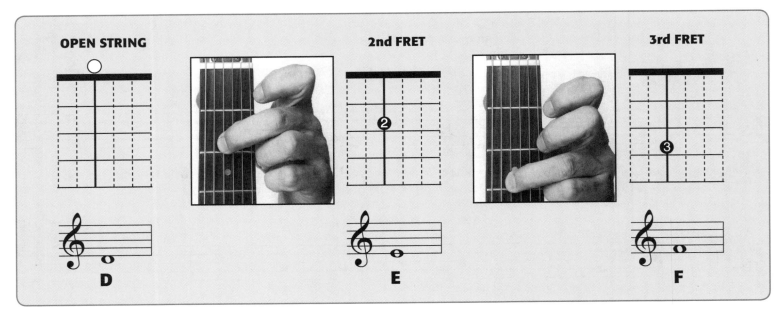

Track 32

OLD MACDONALD HAD A FARM Track 33

Hold Sign (Fermata) 🎵

This sign indicates that the time value of the note is lengthened to approximately twice its usual value.

REUBEN, REUBEN 🔊 Track 34

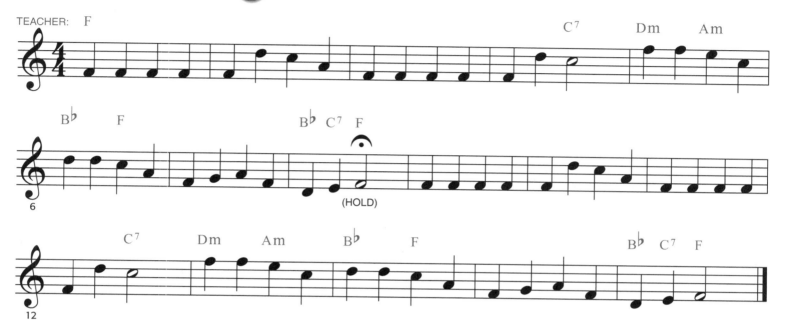

Common Time

𝄴 means *common time*, which is the same as 4/4 time.

G WHIZ 🔊 Track 35

BOHEMIAN FOLK SONG  Track 36

Not all guitar solos are played using one form of the three-note chords already learned.
The next two songs use various combinations of two- and three-note chords.

GOOD NIGHT, LADIES Track 37

Daisy Bell  Track 38
(A Bicycle Built for Two)

Harry Dacre

Four-String G & G7 Chords

The three-note chords you have learned so far can be expanded to four-note chords that sound fuller and richer. For the G and G7 chords, simply add the open 4th string.

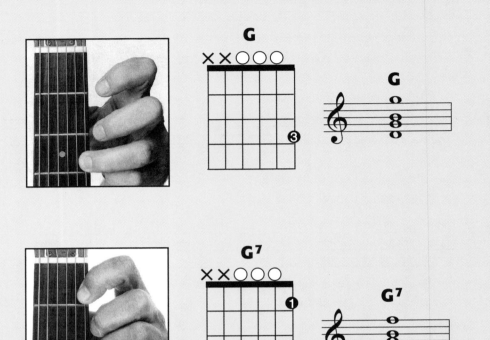

Here is an exercise using expanded four-string versions of the G and G7 chords.

Track 39

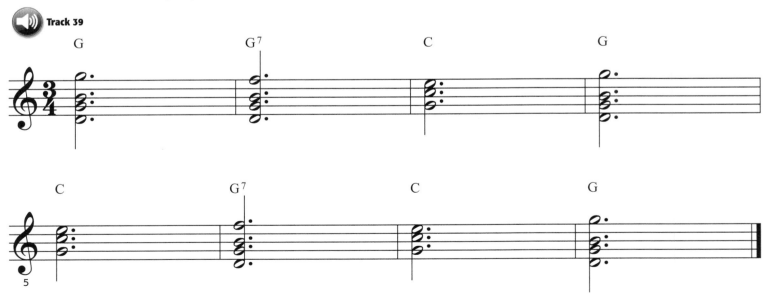

Laughing Polka

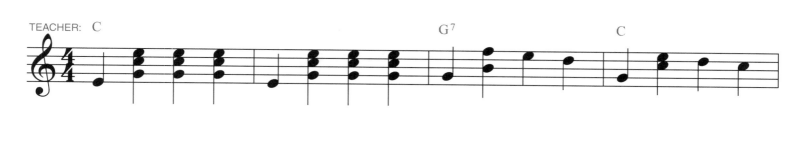

TEACHER:

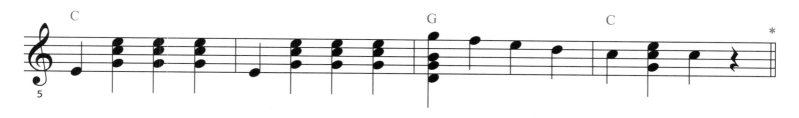

*Two thin lines mean the end of a section.

The Fifth String A

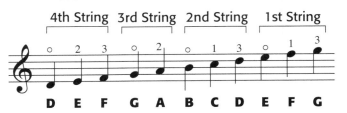

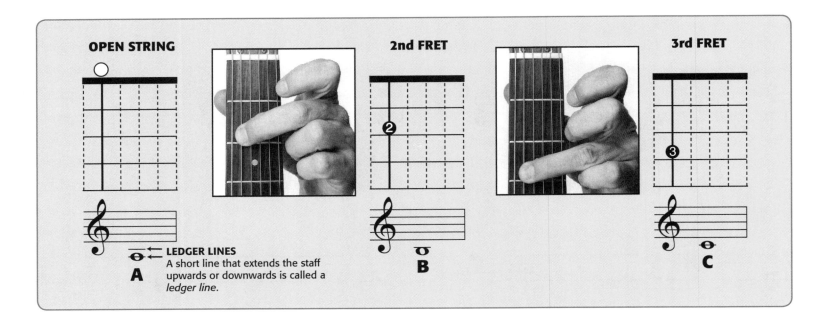

LEDGER LINES
A short line that extends the staff upwards or downwards is called a *ledger line*.

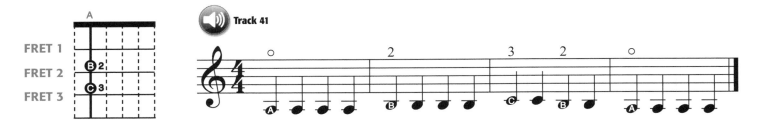

Track 41

VOLGA BOATMEN **Track 42**

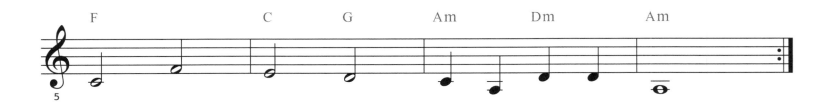

PETER GRAY  Track 43

LOW-DOWN ROCK  Track 44

32

LIEBESTRÄUM  Track 45

Franz Liszt

BOOGIE STYLE Track 46

Introducing High A

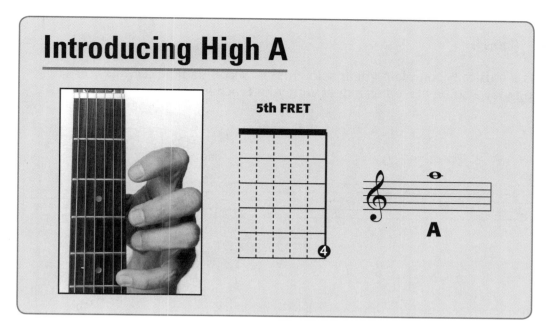

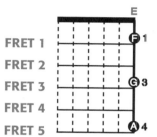

ROCKIN' IN DORIAN MODE Track 48

THE RIDDLE SONG **Track 49**

Play "The Riddle Song" in two ways: as a musically complete guitar solo, then as accompaniment while you sing. Strum chords once each beat. This song may also be played as a duet with your teacher or guitar-playing friend.

Incomplete Measures

Not every piece of music begins on beat 1. Music sometimes begins with an incomplete measure called an *upbeat,* or *pickup.* If the pickup has just one beat, the last measure will have only three beats in $\frac{4}{4}$ or two beats in $\frac{3}{4}$.

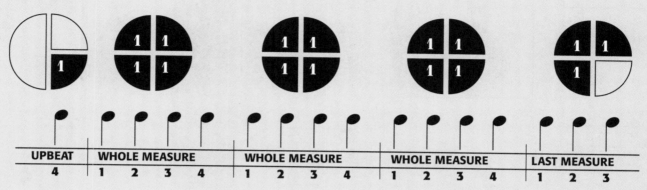

UPBEAT	WHOLE MEASURE	WHOLE MEASURE	WHOLE MEASURE	LAST MEASURE
4	1 2 3 4	1 2 3 4	1 2 3 4	1 2 3

A-TISKET, A-TASKET Track 50

TEACHER:

COUNT: 4

THE YELLOW ROSE OF TEXAS Track 51

TEACHER: G⁷

COUNT: 3 4

The Sixth String E

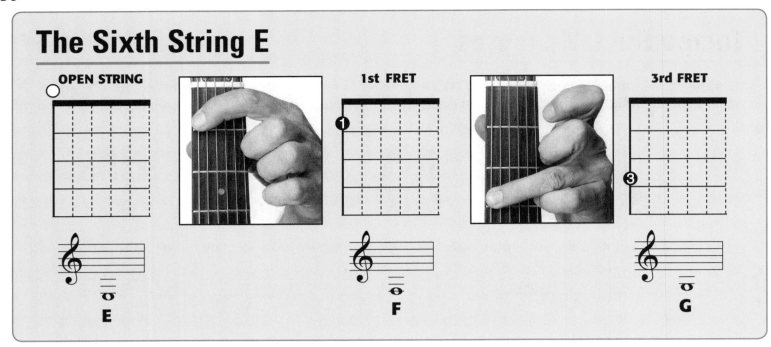

OPEN STRING   **1st FRET**   **3rd FRET**

E   F   G

Track 52

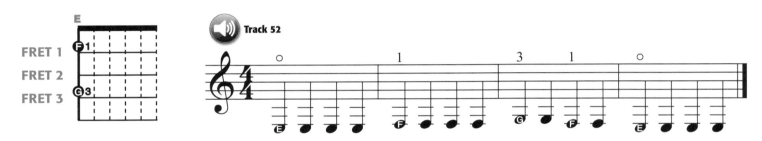

DOWN LOW   **Track 53**

BOTTOM TO TOP   **Track 54**

REVIEW

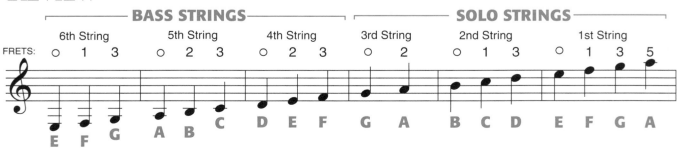

BASS STRINGS   SOLO STRINGS

6th String   5th String   4th String   3rd String   2nd String   1st String

FRETS: ○ 1 3   ○ 2 3   ○ 2 3   ○ 2   ○ 1 3   ○ 1 3 5

E F G   A B   C D E F   G A   B C D   E F G A

Tempo Signs

The three principal *tempo signs* are
Andante (slow), Moderato (moderately), Allegro (fast).

THREE-TEMPO ROCK Track 55

Play three times: 1st time **Andante**, 2nd time **Moderato**, 3rd time **Allegro**.

THE BLUE DANUBE WALTZ Track 56

Johann Strauss

Bass-Chord Accompaniment

A popular style of playing chord accompaniments in $\frac{4}{4}$ time breaks up the chord into a single note and a smaller chord. Play only the lowest note (called the *bass note*) on the 1st beat, then play the rest of the chord on the 2nd, 3rd, and 4th beats.

The complete pattern is **bass-chord-chord-chord**. A variation of this repeats the bass note on the third beat: **bass-chord-bass-chord.**

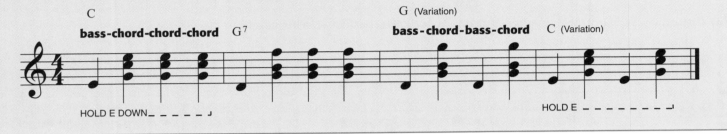

Can-Can (duet) Track 57

This song is a duet. The 1st and 2nd parts are to be played by the student.
The teacher may accompany the student by playing the 2nd part and vice versa.
Follow this procedure on subsequent duets unless otherwise indicated.

Note: The 2nd part is written in bass-chord-chord-chord style
but can also be played in bass-chord-bass-chord style.

Jacques Offenbach

Dynamics

Signs showing how soft or loud to play are called *dynamics*.
The principal dynamics are shown here:

p (piano) soft   *mf* (mezzo-forte) moderately loud   *f* (forte) loud   *ff* (fortissimo) very loud

ECHO WALTZ 🔊 Track 58

Moderato

TEACHER:

Signs of Silence

Stop the sound of the strings by touching them lightly with the heel of your hand.

QUARTER REST = 1 COUNT

HALF REST = 2 COUNTS

WHOLE REST = 4 COUNTS IN 4/4 TIME

3 COUNTS IN 3/4 TIME

THE DESERT SONG (DUET) 🔊 Track 59

(Study in Counting)

ECHO ROCK  Track 60

Two tempo signs may be combined. **Allegro moderato** means "moderately fast."

SHE'LL BE COMIN' 'ROUND THE MOUNTAIN 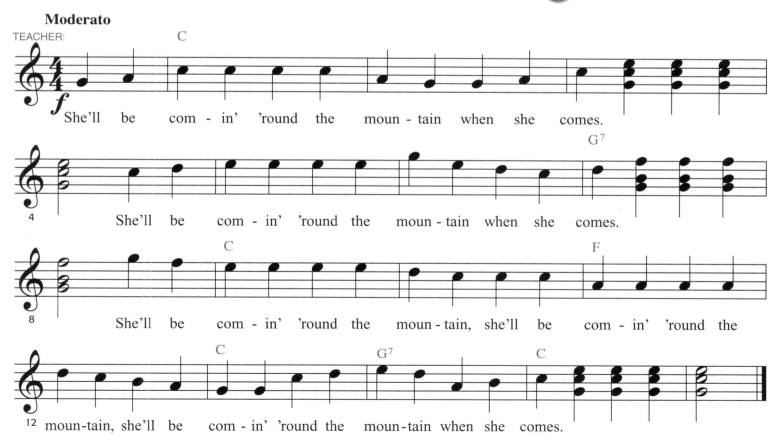 Track 61

Four-String C Chord

The four-string C chord requires placing the 2nd finger on the 2nd fret of the 4th string.

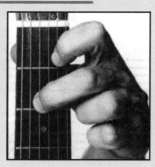
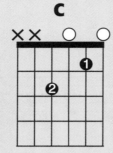
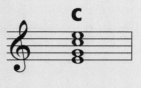

Ties

A *tie* is a curved line that connects two or more notes of the same pitch. When two notes are tied, the second one is not played; rather, the value is added to the first note.

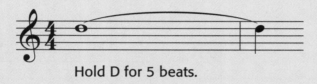

Hold D for 5 beats.

WHEN THE SAINTS GO MARCHING IN (DUET OR TRIO)

Allegro

TEACHER:

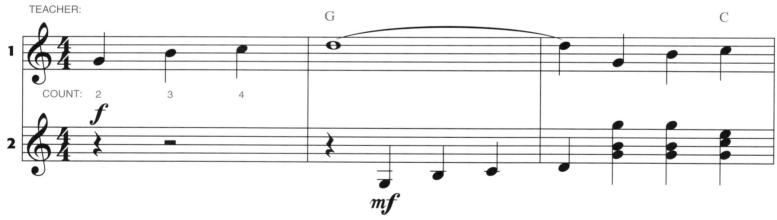

COUNT: 2   3   4

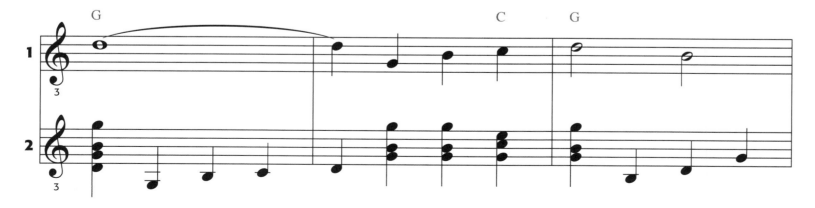

More Bass-Chord Accompaniments

When a piece is in $\frac{3}{4}$ time, a popular style of chord accompaniment is **bass-chord-chord**.
The bass note is the note that names the chord (C for the C chord, G for the G and G7 chords, etc.).
Usually, the bass note is also the lowest note in the chord. First play the bass note alone,
then the rest of the chord on the second and third beats.

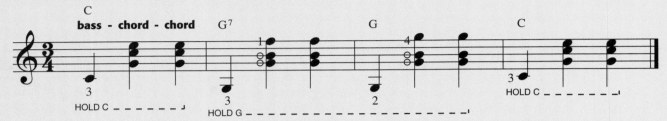

If a chord is repeated for two or more measures, an alternate bass note
(another note in the chord) is used to get a greater variety of sound.

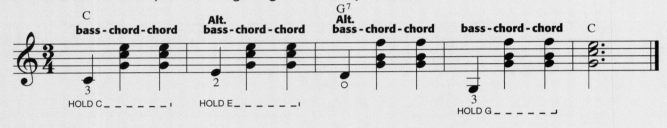

CHIAPANECAS (DUET) Track 63

Mexican Handclapping Song

*Alternate fingering.

Eighth Notes

Eighth notes are black notes with a flag added to the stem: ♪ or ♩.

Two or more eighth notes are written with beams: ♫ or ♫ , ♬ or ♬ .
Each eighth note receives one half beat.

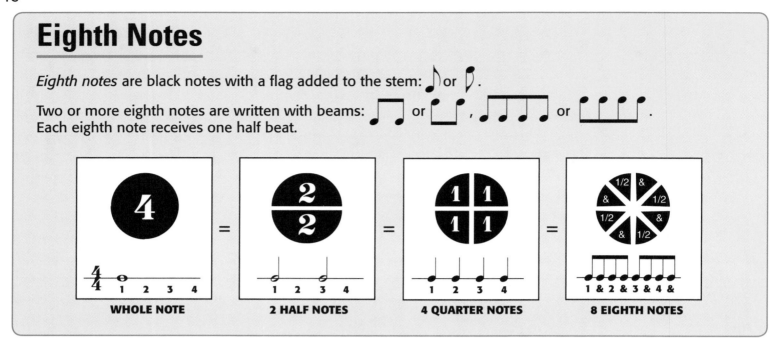

| WHOLE NOTE | 2 HALF NOTES | 4 QUARTER NOTES | 8 EIGHTH NOTES |

Use alternating down-strokes ⊓ and up-strokes V on eighth notes.

Track 64

COUNT: 1 & 2 & 3 & 4 & 1 & 2 & 3 & 4 &

DOWN UP DOWN UP

HAPPY BIRTHDAY TO YOU   Track 65

Mildred J. Hill
and Patty S. Hill

Moderato

TEACHER:

Hap-py birth - day to you. Hap-py birth - day to you. Hap-py

5 birth - day dear _____. Hap - py birth - day to you.
(name)

EIGHTH-NOTE BOUNCE   Track 66

Allegro moderato

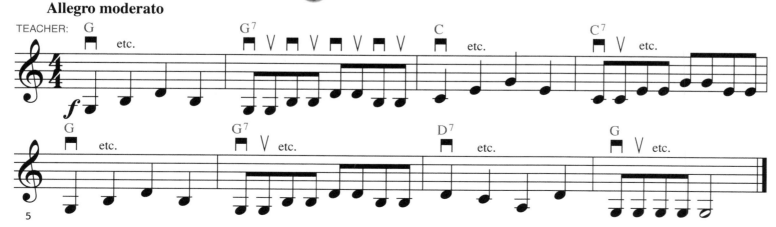

WALKIN' BASS ROCK Track 67

Allegro moderato

More Dynamic Signs

The sign ⦗⟨⦘ and the word *crescendo* both mean grow gradually **louder**.

The sign ⦗⟩⦘ and the word *decrescendo* both mean grow gradually **softer**.

PACHELBEL'S CANON (DUET) Track 68

Play as a round. First player plays as usual. Second player begins when first player gets to Ⓐ.

Johann Pachelbel

Slow and stately

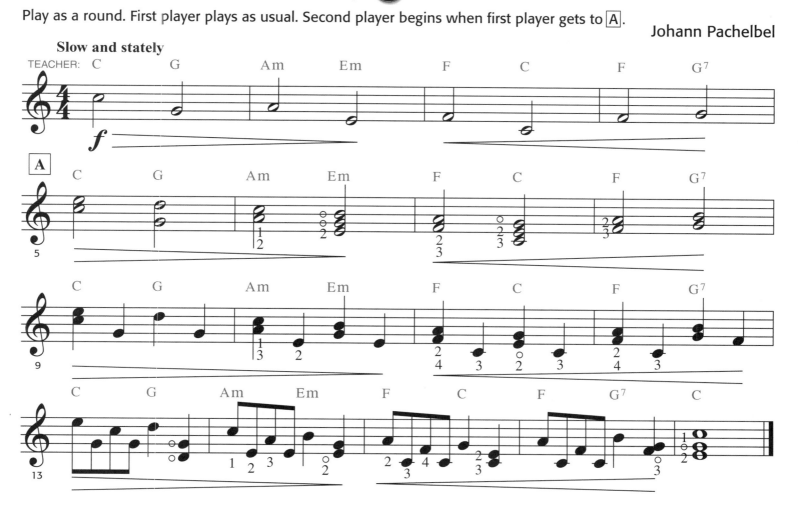

ANNIE'S SONG (DUET)

Track 69

This arrangement can be used several different ways: the 1st part is a self-contained guitar solo;
the 2nd part can be used to accompany your singing. The student should learn both parts.

John Denver

Sharps ♯, Flats ♭, and Naturals ♮

The distance from one fret to the next fret, up or down, is a *half step.* Two half steps make a *whole step.*

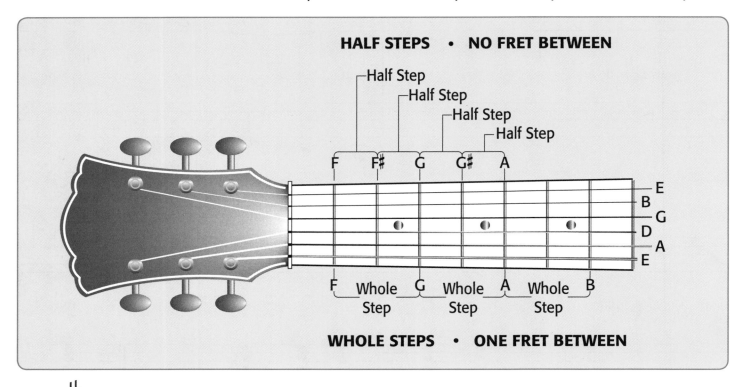

♯ SHARPS **raise** the note a half step. Play the next fret higher.

♭ FLATS **lower** the note a half step. If the note is fingered, play the next fret lower.

> If the note is open, play the 4th fret of the next lower string—except if that string is **G** (3rd string), then play the 3rd fret.

♮ NATURALS **cancel** a previous sharp or flat.

When added within a measure, sharps, flats, and naturals are called *accidentals.*
A bar line cancels a previous accidental in the measures that follow.

The Chromatic Scale Track 70

The *chromatic scale* is formed exclusively of half steps. The ascending chromatic scale uses sharps ♯.
The descending chromatic scale uses flats ♭.

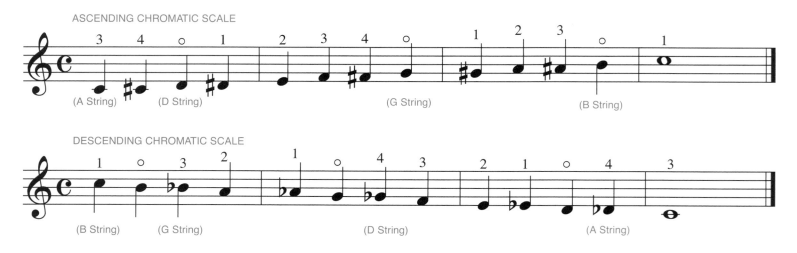

CHROMATIC ROCK  Track 71

MY MELANCHOLY BABY Track 72

*When a sharped or flatted note appears more than once in the same measure, the repeated note is still played sharp or flat unless cancelled by a natural.

A bar line cancels a previous accidental in the measures that follow.

Over the Rainbow

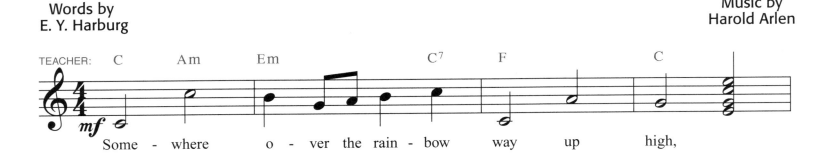 Track 73

Words by
E. Y. Harburg

Music by
Harold Arlen

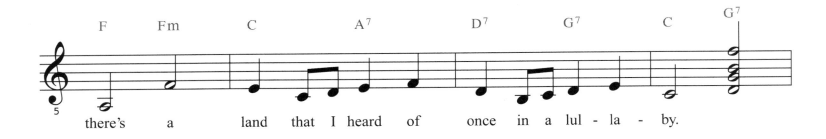

Some - where   o - ver the rain - bow   way   up   high,

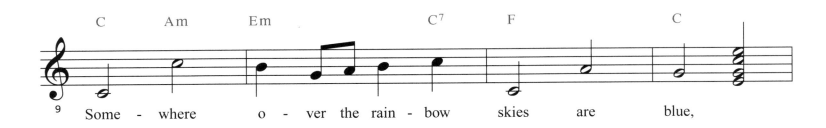

there's   a   land   that I heard of   once in a lul - la - by.

Some - where   o - ver the rain - bow   skies   are   blue,

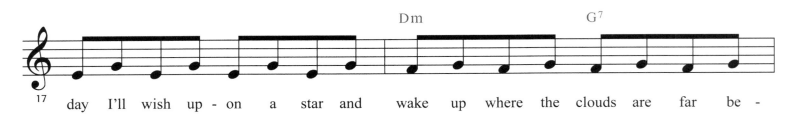

and   the   dreams that you dare to   dream real - ly do come   true.   Some -

day I'll wish up - on   a   star and   wake   up where the clouds are   far   be -

53

hind me._____ Where trou - bles melt like lem - on drops, a -

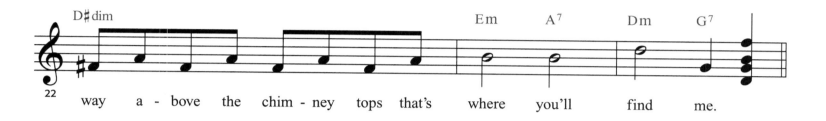

way a - bove the chim - ney tops that's where you'll find me.

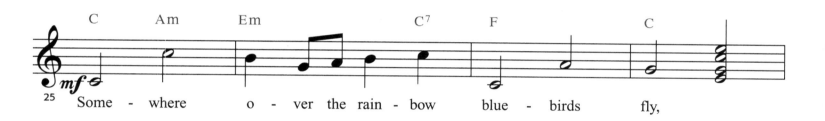

Some - where o - ver the rain - bow blue - birds fly,

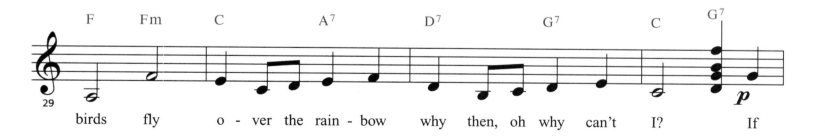

birds fly o - ver the rain - bow why then, oh why can't I? If

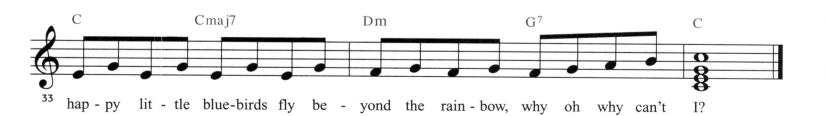

hap - py lit - tle blue-birds fly be - yond the rain - bow, why oh why can't I?

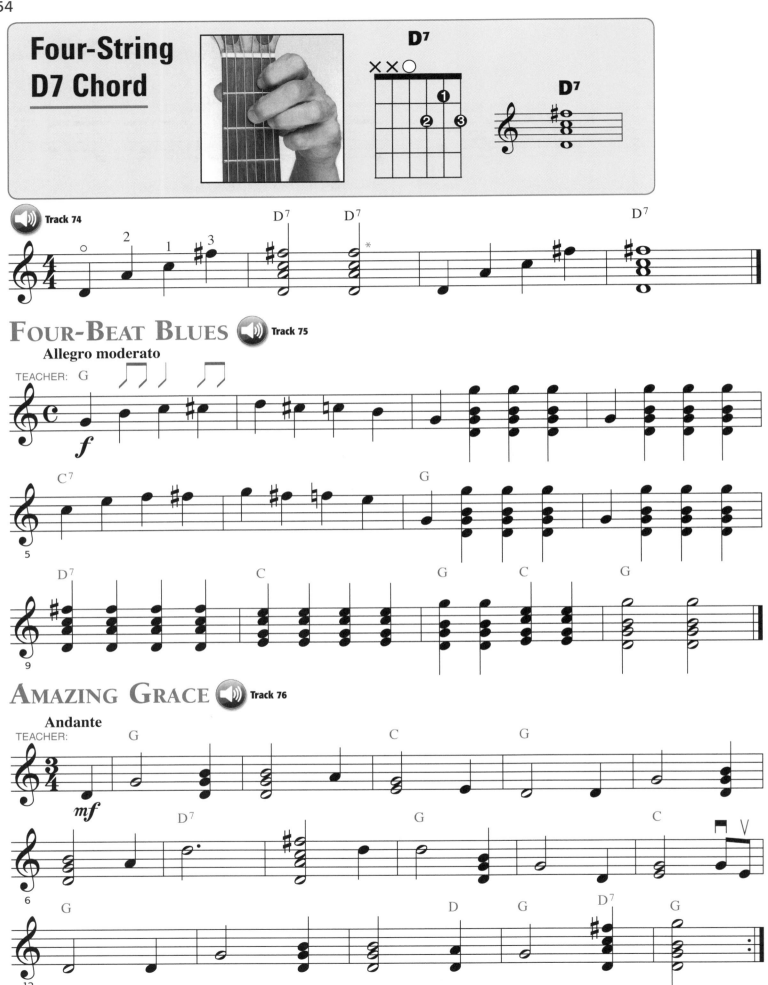

Four-String D7 Chord

D7

Track 74

D7 D7 D7

FOUR-BEAT BLUES Track 75

Allegro moderato

TEACHER: G

C7 G

D7 C G C G

AMAZING GRACE Track 76

Andante

TEACHER: G C G

mf D7 G C

G D G D7 G

*The second F in this measure is also sharp. Accidental sharps, flats, and naturals affect every note on the same line or space but only in the measure in which they appear.

Rockin' the Bach  Track 77

Adapted from a Bach Minuet

Buffalo Gals  Track 78

Play "Buffalo Gals" in two ways: first as a musically complete guitar solo, then as accompaniment while you sing. Strum chords once each beat.

The Major Scale

A *scale* is a succession of eight notes in alphabetical order. All *major scales* are built in the same form:
whole step, whole step, half step,
whole step, whole step, whole step, half step.

The highest note of the scale, having the same letter name as the first note, is called the *octave* note.

C Major Scale

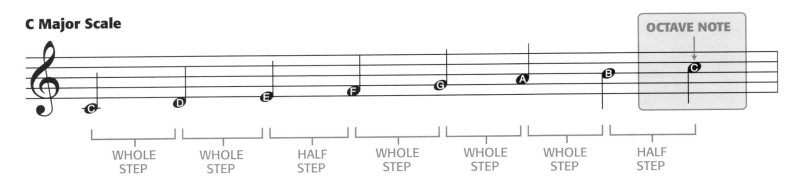

WHOLE STEP	WHOLE STEP	HALF STEP	WHOLE STEP	WHOLE STEP	WHOLE STEP	HALF STEP

It is easier to visualize whole steps and half steps on a piano keyboard. Notice there are whole steps between every natural note except E–F and B–C.

Whole steps - One key between

Half steps - No key between

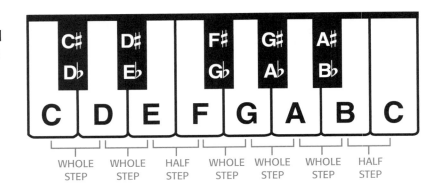

A major scale may be built starting on any note, whether natural, sharp, or flat.
Using the pattern, write a major scale starting on G.

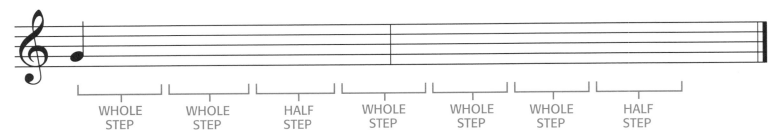

Using the pattern, write a major scale starting on F.

Check: Are the notes in alphabetical order?

Key Signatures

THE KEY OF C MAJOR

A piece based on the C major scale is in the *key of C major.*

THE KEY OF G MAJOR

A piece based on the G major scale is in the *key of G major.* Since F is sharp in the G scale, every F will be sharp in the key of G major. Instead of making all the F's sharp in the piece, the sharp is indicated at the beginning in the *key signature.* Sharps or flats shown in the key signature are effective throughout the piece.

Key Signature
One Sharp (F♯)

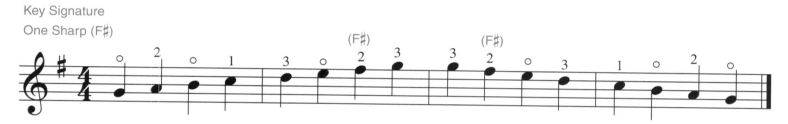

THE KEY OF F MAJOR

A piece based on the F major scale is in the *key of F major.* Since B is flat in the F scale, every B will be flat in the key of F major.

Key Signature
One Flat (B♭)

Accidentals

If sharps, flats, or naturals not shown in the key signature occur in the piece, they are called *accidentals.* Accidentals are effective only for the measures in which they appear.

The three scales shown above should be practiced every day. Students who do this will have little difficulty playing selections written in C major, G major, and F major.

Eighth Rests

 This is an *eighth rest*.
It means to rest for the value of an eighth note.

Single eighth notes are often used with eighth rests:

COUNT: 1   &

Clap or tap the following rhythm:

COUNT: 1   &   2   &   3   &   4   &

EIGHTH REST EXERCISE NO. 1 Track 79

When playing a fingered note, the sound is cut off by releasing the pressure
of the finger on the string. When playing an open note, the sound is cut off
by touching the string with either a left hand finger or the side (heel) of the right hand.

COUNT: 1 & 2 & 3 & 4 &   etc.

EIGHTH REST EXERCISE NO. 2 Track 80

Eighth rests may also appear on downbeats. This creates no problem
if the student marks the downbeat by tapping the foot or mentally counting.

COUNT: 1 & 2 & 3 & 4 &   etc.

EIGHTH REST EXERCISE NO. 3 Track 81

COUNT: 1 & 2 & 3   4   1 & 2 & 3   4   1 & 2 & 3   4   1 & 2 & 3 & 4

BILL BAILEY  Track 82

Moderate ragtime tempo

H. Cannon

* Two counts to a measure—a quarter note gets one count.

LA BAMBA  Track 83

Allegro moderato

Dotted Quarter Notes

A DOT INCREASES THE LENGTH OF A NOTE BY ONE HALF.

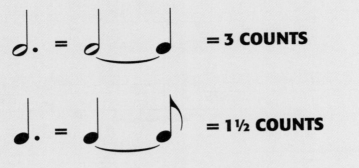 = 3 COUNTS

= 1½ COUNTS

Preparatory Drill

1 & 2 & 3 & 4 &   1 & 2 & 3 & 4 &   1 & 2 & 3 & 4 &

The only difference in the following two measures and those directly above them is the way they are written. They should sound the SAME.

1 & 2 & 3 & 4 &   1 & 2 & 3 & 4 &

AULD LANG SYNE 🔊 Track 84

Singin' in the Rain

Track 85

Lyric by
Arthur Freed

Music by
Nacio Herb Brown

Take Me Home, Country Roads (duet)  Track 86

This country classic is arranged as a duet. The student should learn both parts.

Words and Music by
Bill Danoff, Taffy Nivert,
and John Denver

D.S. al Fine means repeat back to the 𝄋 (*dal segno* sign), then play until the word *Fine*, which indicates the end.

CERTIFICATE OF PROMOTION

ALFRED'S BASIC
GUITAR METHOD 1

This certifies that

_____

has mastered
Alfred's Basic Guitar Method 1
and is promoted to
Alfred's Basic Guitar Method 2

Teacher _____

Date _____